I0411169

CHOOSING TO MAINTAIN CONTROL OF MY LIFE

Steve J. Leatherwood, MA, LPC, NCC

Licensed Professional Counselor

National Board Certified Counselor

ISBN - 10: 1537642367
ISBN-13: 978-1537642369

i

DEDICATION

This book is dedicated to the following people, without whom I could never have made it this far and certainly never have been as blessed as I am without their input, love and support.

To my Wife Dotty, who has been by my side since we were kids in 1962 as a life-long sweetheart, partner and spouse. I can't imagine what would have become of me without her in my life.

To my Sons, J.T. (Jeff) and Jeremy who have been such joys in my life for playtime, music and family time.

To my high school Band Director (and later on adopted grandfather), Ronald C. Muench, who shared music, meals and mentoring with me and always said, "You should write a book!"

To my dear friend, music partner, medical doctor and writing consultant, Dr. Robert (Bobby) Jones, Jr. who inspired me to write something every day and who often shared writings with me.

To my BFF, music partner and morning coffee connoisseur, Dr. Stan Norman, who made fun music and jokes with me, ate 'tater soup and drank coffee as we laughed and watched the sun rise.

And, most importantly to my MOM, Wilda J. Leatherwood, who was the strongest but most gentle, kind and loving mother a little kid could have. She took over when my Father died and I was six years old. She became both Mom and Dad to me. She always trusted me, allowed me to take risks and taught me about respect and gratitude as we sat on the front porch of our home and listed the 'things we were grateful for' many cool evenings in the N.C. mountains years ago.

It is such a GIFT to have friends, supporters, teachers, mentors, companions and family like this along the way to becoming a person. I grew up in a small town where everyone knew everyone and the community "raised" the kids. I was one of those kids. Without the people above and many, many others, I often wonder who I would have become. I am truly blessed.

"For only the hand of Life can contain your hearts. And stand together, yet not too near together: For the pillars of the temple stand apart, And the oak tree and the cypress grow not in each other's shadow."
— **Kahlil Gibran**, **The Prophet**

CONTENTS

CHINESE PROVERB: And the student asks, "Master, where is it that I can find the path to happiness?" And, the Master replies, "Oh, my son, there is NO path to happiness. Happiness lies within the one who walks upon the path." Author Unknown

PREFACE & FOREWORD

I have talked to myself (and others) for years about writing a book. I have written some pages and chapters now and then and stored them on my computer. But, aside from some short journal articles, a book never appeared. However, I recently attended a workshop led by Dr. Robert E. Wubbolding about REALITY THERAPY. If I get a chance to sit in with a workshop or session at a conference with Dr. Wubbolding, it is always high on my list. I became acquainted with Dr. Wubbolding some years ago at a Glasser Institute training week in Copper Mountain, Colorado. We were there to dip into the Glasser pool of knowledge once again and Glasser was there to keep a watchful eye on our efforts. Attending this conference once again reminded me that I had a book to write and it was about some combination of knowledge gained from all the people mentioned in the ACKNOWLEDGEMENTS section of this book.

I suppose that much of my counseling style began to center around Reality Therapy along with a mixture of Person Centered Therapy (Rogers) which I experienced with Dr. C. H. Patterson. When I added in a process style learned from Dr. Sidney Simon with a touch of "Invitational Counseling" from Dr. William Purkey, I came to realize my personal model for helping others.

This is a simple book written by a simple person who enjoys simple things and pleasures. It is written as an effort to help individuals choose to MAINTAIN control of their lives. CHOOSING sounds simple but, as you have already found in your life, choosing is NOT always EASY. And maintenance is the ultimate key. As we grow, our choices will shape and impact our personal and professional lives. The "chapters" in this book are meant to be 'stand alone' readings so that a reader can choose one chapter and get a message without having to read the whole book or without reading the chapters all in order. Thanks for reading in advance. Enjoy YOUR LIFE! And CHOOSE wisely. Choose and Maintain: TO DO or NOT TO DO. Essentially, there is nothing in between.

Two roads DIVERGED IN A WOOD,
AND I, I TOOK THE *one*
LESS TRAVELED BY.
And that HAS MADE *all the difference.*
ROBERT FROST

1 - CHOOSING HOW TO READ THIS BOOK

This may seem like something odd to include in an introduction to a book. But, some people, like me for instance, don't always read a book 'cover to cover' starting with the first page. However, that is one way to read or use this book but there are others. So let me expand on the options.

- OPTION 1: You could, as suggested above, choose to read the book "cover to cover" starting with the first page and continuing to the end. That is the way most books are designed to be read and the way most people (I suppose) read books. So that is OPTION 1: Cover to Cover, Start to Finish. Beginning to End.
- OPTION 2: In addition to the above choice of how to use this book, consider this: check out the list of "chapters" and see if some particular one strikes your fancy and choose that one to read. It can be anywhere in the book as this book is not particularly designed to be in any particular sequence and each 'chapter' is a 'stand-alone' reading. While the chapters have some references to each other, and may mention thoughts or techniques from another chapter, they are not written to be dependent on each other.
- OPTION 3: Finally, if you want, you can just open the book to a page, preferably the beginning of a chapter (that probably should be a starting point) and just take a 'pot-luck' version of what might be discussed in that chapter.
- FINAL NOTE: In addition to the above ways to choose how to read this book, it might also be true that you will find certain chapters more appealing to you and you may want to mark them to re-read in the future (I HOPE!). This book

is meant to be a 'book of readings' more that a 'book to read' so if you find some information that is particularly significant to you and your life, family or work, you can read that several times or as a refresher to the concept discussed.

At any rate, I sincerely hope that you enjoy reading this material and my thoughts. Thanks in advance for taking the time to share some moments with me and these ideas. And, most importantly, I hope that you will find something here that will make your day, work, family, relationship, and/or life just a little better or easier.

I would love to hear from you and you are welcome to drop me a note to the following addresses:

Steve J. Leatherwood, PO Box 699, Shelby, NC 28151-0699

2 - CHOOSING SIMPLE

I have been convinced that SIMPLE may be the secret to change. Complicated is not the secret. Complications just lead to postponements, excuses and stagnation. Simple is what this book is about. Let me explain simple. I remember as a child being told that something was "easy as 1-2-3" or "simple as A-B-C" and maybe there is more truth to that old adage than we care to believe. Most times, it seems that only a few steps lead to success. In my learning about being a counselor, there were often complex theories to digest and detailed diagrams to follow and apply to helping clients change.

But, I have come to believe that it is really not necessary to follow a complex pattern of maps and puzzles to reach a realistic solution to problems. In fact, as I have heard it said, "Clients don't really have problems...they have solutions that are not working." And that seems to be the answer in a nutshell. It's not that one has an unsolvable problem, only a solution to a problem that is not working. All that is needed is another solution that might work if applied to the situation. If we discard that solution and control our thinking to "look outside the box" for another possible solution (or solutions) that might work, we can change from road blocked to smooth sailing with a new, workable solution.

In working with teachers, I often used a version of this phrase, "Continue to teach the same material in the same way and you will continue to get the same results". If your classroom or students seem to be moving in a direction you do not want, is it fair to assume that things will just 'get better' if you keep doing what you have always done? Probably, that is not a responsible choice. If we expect change to occur, we have to be willing to change our thinking and/or acting. Acting or thinking in the same way will most likely get the same results. Funny how that works!

So, back to the 1-2-3 or A-B-C concept. If we break down our behavior or thinking change into a couple reasonable and manageable steps, we can move through the situation (problem) toward a solution. This is a similar idea to the READY, FIRE, AIM concept in shooting a gun. If one continues this behavior, most likely it will be difficult to actually hit a target except by sheer luck. So if Step 1 is GET READY, Step 2 is TAKE AIM, and Step 3 is FIRE or TAKE ACTION, maybe we could be more effective.

An important learning I had many years ago came to me by way of Dr. Sidney Simon who told of a woman whose name was Dr. Maymie Porter. She had a simple method for change. You will probably see this again later in this book about change but her questions for change were clear:

1) What are you currently doing that works, or seems to be effective and you like?
2) Now that you have some experience, what do you think you could do differently that might work better if you did it?
3) What do you need to know or possess that would help you get started doing those things you know would work better?

Again, a very SIMPLE way of looking a CHANGE.

Getting READY for a change involves thinking about where we want to be after the change. Looking toward the END RESULT and visualizing what we really, REALLY want to achieve in the end. As simple as this sounds, many individuals fail in their attempts because they do not have a vision of the end result. It is much like looking at a map when you travel. If you want to get from point A to point B, looking at point B is critical to determine the direction of your travel. Then, you can map out what to do between point A and point B to make that trip. Simply starting out in some direction HOPING to get where we want to be seems silly, but it is often what happens. We can't get from Tennessee to California if we travel east.

FIRST get READY, figure out where we want to be in the end (of a task, a period of time, or event) and visualize that as a GOAL.

SECONDLY, TAKE AIM. By choosing a reasonable and effective direction or behavior as we move toward our goal, we make our chances of success much more attainable.   Taking AIM involves figuring out what will be needed to make the 'trip' to our goal a success. This may be the most difficult of the three steps in that it will involve some planning, consideration, choosing as well as elimination in the preparing process. We have to decide what we want or need to do and what elements might be necessary for us to collect as resources for help along the way. Making a list is often a critical part of being sure all the necessary parts are available to us as we need them. Much like a "grocery list" is important when making a trip to the store, it will help us to do or get what we really NEED or WANT and not forget something essential. How many of us have said, "Oh, I'll remember that" and not write down something important and then get back home to realize we forgot to get the gallon of milk or loaf of bread we needed the most? Make a PLAN and WRITE IT DOWN.

FINALLY: We can ACT on the plan. Taking ACTION on our plan and DOING what we must do to get what we want should be successful. Sometimes, we fail by simply not acting in the way we know would work if we just did it. But, to be successful, that is what it takes – ACTION. Work your PLAN. Start now and don't give up.

So, in summary, change is SIMPLE. One just needs to know where they are and what they are doing, plan for (or change to) a solution that will most likely get what we really want and then act on the plan to get there. It is simple, as said before, but it is not always easy. It does take work and it does take thinking and acting in responsible ways to achieve a goal.

William Glasser's
Choice Theory

We all make choices according to basic needs that come from within ourselves. The needs drive our choices and influence how we behave in those choices.

3 - CHOOSING CHANGE

Speaking of SIMPLE methods to CHANGE, a little over a hundred years ago, William James (1842-1910) a noted psychologist of the time, stated simply that if you wanted to change something in your life, you only needed to do three things. And his thinking was that if you really did this these three things, you could change anything you wanted about yourself, your behavior or your thinking.

Stated simply, his plan was:

- Do it NOW!
- Do it BIG!
- Get Watchers!

Let's look at each one on these three steps.

DO IT NOW!: Doing it NOW means that to change something you need to start now, immediately. Don't put off until after Thanksgiving to start that diet or until after the next party to stop smoking or eating chocolate. But to do it today! Start immediately when you have the thought and don't wait for some magical time or to get past some other event in your life. DO IT NOW!

DO IT BIG!: Secondly, he said that if we want to change we need to also do it BIG. In other words, do whatever you plan to do every day in all parts of your day everywhere you go. Surround yourself with the change and put pictures on the refrigerator and your bathroom mirror to remind yourself of the change. Make yourself notes or signs about the change. Start a calendar or a checklist to keep track of what you are changing and how you are doing. Write notes in a journal about how you are doing each day. Carry the journal with you and make notes throughout the day. Make the change an obvious part of your daily life.

GET WATCHERS: Finally, to be fully effective in achieving your goal of change, you need to recruit others to "watch" you. Let some of your friends, partners, neighbors and co-workers know that you have decided to change. Tell them what you are doing and remind them occasionally that you are working on this change in your life. It is easy to fail if you attempt to make a change in secret. But with people watching you and reminding you that you said you were changing, you develop a support system to give you courage, keep you on track, boost your willpower, and give you positive feedback as they notice the change.

Three simple steps to changing pretty much anything you want to change in your life. Probably another key to the process is that you need to WANT to change before you attempt the change. TALKING about a change and DOING it are two different things and many of us talk a good plan but never put it into action. James' idea is to decide on the change to be made and get on with it! This model has been used by many groups of people who have decided to make changes in their lives. It will work if YOU will work with it. Do it NOW! Do it BIG! Get some WATCHERS! You can change if you simply stick with the plan and I would add, DON'T GIVE UP!

WHEN YOU CHANGE THE WAY YOU LOOK AT THINGS, THE THINGS YOU LOOK AT CHANGE

~dr. wayne dyer

4 - CHOOSING HELPING

Over my professional career, which now spans almost 50 years, only a few things stand out as important to making my work successful, satisfying and fun. This is one of those few things. The concept is rooted in the work of one of my teachers William Glasser, MD and his concepts of Reality Therapy or Choice Theory depending on when you read Glasser's work. It is a relatively simple concept but a most powerful and life-changing model to move from failure to success.

Glasser's theory is based on the ideas of choosing and alternatives and about things that HURT and things that HELP. In short, we have most control over WHAT WE DO and WHAT WE THINK. We have less control over how we FEEL and our PHYSICAL RESPONSE to events.

The central question Glasser proposes in his concept goes like this: "Is what you doing (or thinking) helping you to get what you want (achieve your goal)?" And while this may seem simplistic and obvious as a question, it is in a powerful position to help you take and maintain control of your life, which is what this small book is all about.

Here are just a couple words about WANTS and NEEDS. Some years ago I knew a fellow who said he was drinking too much and he thought drinking had become a problem. The drinking had started in high school, and for some 20-odd years continued every day after work. It was simply work, come home, drink 6-8 pack and go to bed. The next day would repeat it all over again. One key element of importance seemed to be present, however. As we talked the statements were very clear, "I don't NEED to quit drinking….I WANT to quit drinking." Drinking was not creating major problems in his life. Being able to go to work, earn a living and get along reasonably well in the family weren't problems. But, the determining factor was that drinking every day was NOT the way he wanted his life to be forever.

The key to this story is in WANT versus NEED to quit. The workplace didn't have a problem with drinking a 'few beers' as long as a person came to work on time, did their job and didn't create any problems with other workers. That was working. So, NEEDING to quit drinking wasn't the issue. But, drinking was NOT HELPING to achieve his life goals. He was in a rut. Work, drink, sleep - work, drink, sleep. And this person had come to realize that RUT was NOT ENOUGH for his LIFE.

So what we WANT and what we NEED are very different things. We NEED food, water, oxygen and shelter to survive. Our WANTS are often less clear in that we might WANT a steak, some ice cream, a new car, a different job, etc. but these are not essentials for survival. He had decided he no longer WANTED to be a 7 day-a-week drinker. And, as he put it, he didn't "need to quit" but he "wanted to quit". And that's the big difference.

If we decide what we are doing (or thinking) is NOT helping us to achieve our goal or dream, it is time to REJECT that behavior (or thinking) as a HURTING behavior and to then CHOOSE a behavior (or thought) that would be HELPFUL and would steer us in the direction we really WANT to go and toward what we have chosen as our goal.

While this sounds simple, it is not easy to break habitual behaviors or thought patterns that we have practiced for some time, maybe even years. But it is possible to make this simple choice that "what I am doing (thinking) is NOT helping me" and replace that behavior (or thinking) with actions and thoughts that are consistent with what we really, REALLY want. Then we can continue to repeat the NEW behavior or thinking as often as we can until it becomes the habit.

Once we decide what we really, REALLY WANT and are willing to make the commitment to BEHAVE in ways necessary to get what we REALLY WANT, success is easily within our reach. It is always helpful to have support in this process, at least to begin with, but soon we can adopt the HELPFUL behavior and thinking as our NEW way and continue those actions for a more productive and satisfying life.

So, here's the deal. Think about where you want to be in life, sooner or later. Next, think about what you are doing or thinking on a regular basis. NOW, the moment of TRUTH: IS WHAT YOU ARE DOING OR THINKING MOVING YOU TOWARD WHAT YOU REALLY, REALLY WANT? You must be honest with yourself on this one. There is NO IN-BETWEEN, what you do/think is either HELPING or HURTING. PERIOD. It is a two-column list, and EVERYTHING falls on one side or the other.

EXERCISE: Draw a TWO-COLUMN list and title one column HELPING THINGS and the other column HURTING THINGS. Write in as many things as you can on both columns. Then, as you look at the lists, your challenge is to DO MORE of the HELPING things and QUIT or DO FEWER of the HURTING things (maybe eliminate them all together).

If you want, you can draw it right here, in this book, on the next page! I have even started one for you.

"We almost always have choices, and the better the choice, the more we will be in control of our lives." William Glasser **Take Effective Control of Your Life,** xiii Harper & Row, Publ. NY 1984

HELPING   THINGS   vs   HURTING   THINGS

5 - CHOOSING BALANCE

Over the years, I have found the root problem in many counseling situations is often BALANCE – "How much is ENOUGH?" Almost every situation whether it involves an individual, a couple or family involves dealing with BALANCE and usually it is about being OUT of balance. "How can I maintain a balance?" BALANCE lies somewhere between TOO MUCH and TOO LITTLE. We might refer to this concept as similar to "Just Right" like we read about as a child.

As children, we struggle with having to go to school and wanting to play outside. As adults, we struggle with eating all we want at the buffet restaurant and a diet.

BALANCE ISSUES: Consider these. You can't do both in most cases.

WORK TIME vs FAMILY TIME

ALONE TIME vs TIME WITH OTHERS

SLEEP TIME/REST TIME vs EXERCISE TIME

PERSONAL TIME vs TIME WITH SPOUSE or FRIENDS

AND HOW MUCH IS ENOUGH ISSUES: How much do we REALLY need?

WORK TIME, FAMILY TIME, PERSONAL TIME, SLEEP TIME, EATING, DRINKING, TELEVISION, COMPUTER, SOCIAL MEDIA TIME

Let's take look at some main areas in our lives where we need to maintain balance and ways to figure out what is 'ENOUGH'.

MAJOR AREAS: WORK TIME; SLEEP/REST TIME

FIRST: WORK TIME

One of the biggest areas most of us struggle with is WORK. Now, if you don't have to work, that's great!! You can probably skip most of this chapter! But, a large percentage of the population finds it necessary to work some and make money to pay expenses and provide for themselves and their family. Sometimes is very easy to get out of balance in our work time since we do not have total control of how much or when we work. If you work for a person or company, your hours, days and frequency of work are all controlled by that person or company. Also what you get paid is controlled there as well. So we are forced to coordinate our lives around our work time, unless we are 'self-employed' and that might even be WORSE! For the sake of average numbers, let us say that for the majority, a person works about EIGHT hours a day and/or FORTY hours a week.

Balance comes into play sometimes if the more we work, the more money we earn. We can fall into the trap of thinking that MORE is better since we can pay more bills, buy more 'things' and have more cash. But if we work MORE than the average, it comes at the expense of our 'time off' and other ways we might spend our time. So as we think about BALANCE, working versus not working is a critical component that often impacts several, if not all of the other areas.

So let's try a little exercise. Your work time situation might be different if you work 12 hour shifts or 2-day weekends, but you know how many hours you spend and the numbers of 8 and 40 are just an average. Use YOUR work time specifics as you answer the following questions.

- Question: How much time do you work each day? ___
- Question: How much time do you spend getting ready for work (dressing, etc.) each day? ___
- Question: How much time do you spend travelling to and from work each day? ___

SECOND: SLEEP TIME/RESTING TIME: How much is enough?

All of us do need a certain amount of rest and/or sleep daily to be able to function up to our best. Without enough quality, restful sleep, people often become difficult to be around, may be angry or unhappy and will be tired and less productive. Some people spend more time "in bed" but often are not resting or sleeping. And sometimes, we wait for a day off and attempt to 'sleep all day' and catch up. Unfortunately, the body doesn't work well that way and really prefers a regular 6-8 hours of quality sleep time daily.

- Question: How much time do you sleep on a normal day? ___

NOW, let's stop and do some math. If we work about EIGHT hours on a daily basis (you do your math) and we sleep about EIGHT hours on a daily basis, that adds up to about SIXTEEN hours total in a 24-hour day. Remember: earlier we talked about having to get ready for work and travel to and from work so let's add another 2 hours each day to our schedule as we consider BALANCE and time.

So, 8 + 8 + 2 = 18 RIGHT? So, 24 − 18 = 6 RIGHT? That's 24 hours in a day, minus work time, sleep time and preparation/travel time. So we have SIX hours to use for other chores and responsibilities to be "in balance".

OTHER IMPORTANT AREAS: FAMILY TIME, PERSONAL TIME, EXERCISE TIME, PLAY TIME, MEAL TIME, SOCIAL TIME: HOW MUCH IS ENOUGH?

A healthy lifestyle usually includes some time for you personally and with your family members, assuming you have a family, or with friends if you are single. This includes time to talk with your friends, spouse and children, to work on hobbies or to catch up on household chores and duties around the home, and maybe work in a few minutes to read a book or the newspaper, listen to some music or walk the dog! And don't forget breakfast, lunch and dinner! But, that's not all. Since the late 1990's, a NEW AREA has become increasingly 'thirsty' for our time and that is: COMPUTER, CELL PHONE, SOCIAL MEDIA and TV TIME.

- QUESTION: How much time do you spend with your spouse, children, friends or other family members each day? _____
- QUESTION: How much time do you spend with daily/weekly exercise? ____
- QUESTION: How much time to you give yourself to work on personal projects, personal enjoyment and 'play'? _____
- QUESITON: How much time do you spend with meals each day? ____
- QUESTION: How much time each day do you spend with "electronic devices" such as computers, televisions, and cell phones? ____

Well, it is becoming fairly obvious why BALANCE is such a difficult issue for many if not most of us and why we must constantly borrow time from some area to add to another. Unfortunately, we do have that 24-hour limitation on each day, so we have to make our work and tasks all fit that limit.

If you think about these areas for a moment, consider about what you would like to do with your time and how you might like to spend some time. Maybe some time with your children to do homework or listen to their concerns about school. Or, with your friends for a party? Or, with your spouse for dinner and a movie? Maybe you have a hobby or like to garden or work in your yard. STOP and think for a moment about what else you NEED or WANT to do in the SIX hours you have left.

EXERCISE: How would I CHOOSE to spend my time?

(Think about what you would LIKE to do if you had total control over your time. Put some serious thought into this since you DO have control of some hours.)

- QUESTION: How much time would you spend with family/loved ones? ____
- QUESTION: How much time would you spend with music or reading? ____
- QUESTION: How much time would you spend with exercise? ____
- QUESTION: How much time would you spend going to church? ____
- QUESTION: How much time would you spend being with your friends? ____
- QUESTION: How much time would you spend with your hobby? ____
- QUESTION: How much time would you spend with TV, social media? ____
- QUESTION: What other things could you CHOOSE to spend time doing during your day? (include the time you would like to spend)

○ _____

○ _____

○ _____

○ _____

○ _____

○ _____

SOME CONSIDERATIONS ABOUT OTHER AREAS:

EATING: (Food & Beverages) Of course, we have to fuel for our body to be able to work, play and simply stay alive on a daily basis. Our work schedule may dictate some about our EATING schedule both in timing and menu since we may have to 'eat on the run' (although we probably should not do that often). And what about our diet? We planned to lose some weight and eat better quality meals.

FAMILY TIME: While it is important for us to plan a good, balanced diet for our self and for our family and also to work toward a regular plan for meal times, it is difficult at times. Families in past times usually had an evening meal together, Sunday dinners with the grandparents, and breakfast every day before going out to work. In more recent years, that concept has been forced to change to conform to shift work, school events, and other activities and duties. A "date-night" for dinner with your spouse or watching a movie at home with the whole family could be well spent time. We promised a family vacation trip but when will we do that? Important events if we want to stay in balance but not necessarily easy to accomplish!

TV, CELL PHONE and COMPUTER TIME: Studies have suggested that even 15 years ago, around the year 2000 and before, the average person was spending 5-6 hours a day watching television. Families in past times were not as influenced by computer and internet (much less CELL PHONES) to compete for their time. But now this area becomes a major challenge when we consider balancing our time.

Believe it or not, the most prevalent issue today in couple, family and relationship counseling is the CELL PHONE and social media. We are becoming increasingly dependent upon and tied to our cell phones to the point that we text and email while having lunch with our spouse, while watching TV or even at work. Many youths I know constantly have their phone in their hand much of the day if people will allow that in school, or at home. Computers, social media and cell phones continue to drive wedges between relationships and in some cases, have prevented them from forming at all.

Choosing this balancing and assigning of the time 'left' is often where individuals run into trouble. Our work time is pretty much forced into place and we have little or no control of that in most cases. Sleep is pretty much the same situation although we do find that many people carve out minutes or hours of sleep time to do other things. We have to take some time to eat and to travel to and from work. How will we ever get it all worked into our 24-hour day?

We are faced with dividing up SIX hours between family, friends, children, spouse, recreation, eating, and electronic devices (social media) and this is where the real IMBALANCE often occurs. Not ENOUGH time for FAMILY, FRIENDS, SELF, SPOUSE, CHILDREN, and now, since the late 1990s, we have been forced to deal with the constant presence of not only television, but more intrusively, cell phones, texting, email and social media. While these can be very helpful in our lives and even great ways to communicate more easily, they do take over an increasing amount of time in our lives.

Dividing up the remaining precious SIX hours is quite a chore. Do I spend time with my family, my children, my loved ones, or do I selfishly take time for myself to work on hobbies or do something I 'want to do'? Do I help the kids with their homework? And, who's cleaning up the house and cooking meals and doing all the other chores?

It is clearly a struggle to CHOOSE how to spend your 24 hours each day, BUT we do only get 24 hours to work with and must face the challenge of providing ENOUGH time for the important things in our life. NOW the question becomes, "What is really important enough for me to CHOOSE to spend time doing? What do I REALLY, REALLY want to do and need to do?"

REMEMBER: Balance is the KEY. How much is "JUST RIGHT"? How much is TOO MUCH? And how much is TOO LITTLE? Do we need ANY of it at all? Could you cut some time from one area to spend more time in another? It is SIMPLE but it is NOT easy! It is a constant struggle to "balance" time and to keep it in our favor so that we hold stress to a minimum and enjoy our lives to the maximum. It is a never-ending challenge, finding ENOUGH.

So where do we assign the time we have left. REMEMBER: We only get 24 hours in each day! Balance is something we constantly struggle to maintain. Once we think we have everything covered, something will change and we have to start all over.

YOUR ASSIGNMENT: Since you do not have much control over work and travel time, and your body forces you to sleep some time, your question now is: How do I CHOOSE to spend the rest of my 24 hours? Go to the AVERAGE DAILY TIME WORKSHEET at the end of this chapter. DO YOUR BEST BALANCING ACT! Remember, ENOUGH is somewhere between TOO MUCH and TOO LITTLE. Not to hot, not too cold, JUST RIGHT! If we work that to our advantage, we can have and do most of the things that are important to our self, our family, and our friends.

EXERCISE: Write in <u>actual times you would schedule</u> for events in a regular day.

MY AVERAGE DAILY SCHEDULE

WORK TIME: _____

PREPARATION TIME/TRAVEL TIME: _____

SLEEP TIME/REST TIME: _____

MEAL TIME: Breakfast: _____ Lunch: _____ Dinner: _____

OTHER EVENTS/ACTIVITIES:

     1. _____
     2. _____
     3. _____

     TOTAL TIME INVOLVED: _____

WRITE ABOUT BALANCE ISSUES YOU HAVE IN YOUR LIFE

WHAT IS DIFFICULT FOR YOU TO BALANCE?

WHERE DO YOU NEED MORE TIME?

WHERE COULD YOU SPEND LESS TIME?

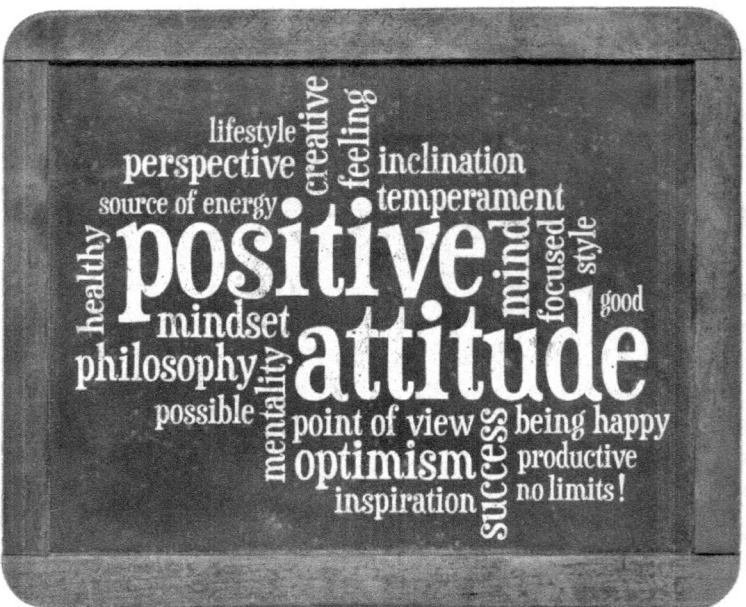

6 - CHOOSING ATTITUDE

I have often heard it said that a person "got an attitude with me" meaning something negative between the people in most cases. Where did they 'get' that attitude? We do seem to carry 'attitudes' toward things or people. Do we "choose" those attitudes? Roberto Assagioli, MD, (1888–1974) a renowned psychiatrist and psycho-synthesis therapist who helped hundreds of people sort out problems in their lives, helped by doing this simple thing. He asked people to hold to a single attitude he called "the Attitude of Gratitude" in their lives. He went on to say that people could hold many different attitudes in their lives. The attitude of dissatisfaction, of superiority, of anger, and of impatience as well as many others are possible but might be found quite ineffective in having and maintaining relationships with others. The list of possibilities is almost endless.

However, Roberto suggests that one single, simple attitude of being grateful, having gratitude, would sustain anyone in their journey through life. To simply choose such an attitude would, in fact, feed our relationship with others, with our work, and with our personal self. If we chose to look around each day and speak of the gratitude we feel for the people, blessings and achievements in our lives, we would live happier and more contented lives.

Activities of the attitude of gratitude are simple as well. One simply voices the words of gratitude toward people and events for which they are grateful. Choosing your children or your spouse as objects of gratitude might be a good place to start. When did you last speak to your spouse of your gratitude to them for being part of your life and the same of your children? How grateful are you for the blessings you have received in your work and play? And, your friends or co-workers, are you grateful for their presence in your life?

Making a list of your 'gratitudes' would be a great personal activity and sharing that list with others, even more fulfilling. My mother often sat with me on our front porch and said, "Let's talk about what we are grateful for" and we did just that. I remember it well and it was a pleasant and uplifting exchange for us. Grateful for the birds and flowers, for wind and rain, for music and love, for sight and hearing, for each other, for so many things often taken for granted.

In Roberto's words, "Of all the attitudes we can hold (and we do hold attitudes about the people around us) the greatest of these is the attitude of gratitude". Roberto Assagioli (1888–1974)

I would challenge you to find and choose a greater attitude than the Attitude of Gratitude.

EXERCISE: Make a list below of all the things for which you are grateful. You can start the list and come back later as you think of other things. Ask your family members to consider this and especially your children. In working with people over the years, it seems that 'gratitude' has faded somewhat and sometimes we find people who seem not to be grateful for much of anything.

Maybe it is up to us, each and every one, to rekindle the Attitude of Gratitude in ourselves and in others we know. It can start with us and a single act of Gratitude, if we CHOOSE to do that.

MY LIST OF THINGS FOR WHICH I AM GRATEFUL: (just keep numbering and use other pages if needed)

1. I am grateful for

_____

2. I am grateful for

_____

3. I am grateful for

_____

4. I am grateful for

_____

5. I am grateful for

_____

6. I am grateful for

_____

7. I am grateful for

_____

8. I am grateful for

_____

9. I am grateful for

_____

10. I am grateful for

_____

11. I am grateful for

_____

12. I am grateful for

_____

13. I am grateful for

_____

14. I am grateful for

_____

15. I am grateful for

_____

16. I am grateful for

_____

17. I am grateful for

_____

18. I am grateful for

_____

19. I am grateful for

_____

20. I am grateful for

_____

21. I am grateful for

_____

22. I am grateful for

_____

23. I am grateful for

_____

24. I am grateful for

_____

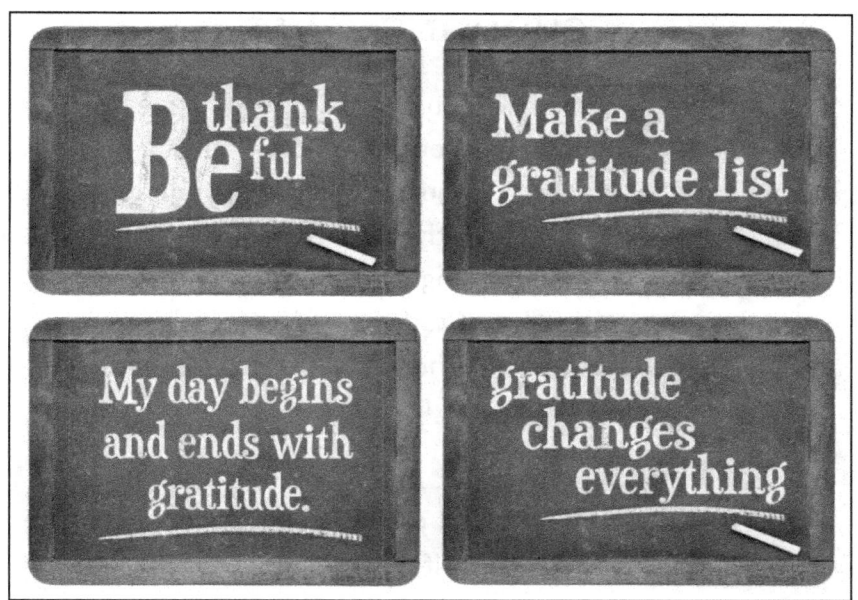

7 - CHOOSING LANGUAGE

Over the years, I have had a number of influential mentors, educators and friends who spoke about the "language" we use to communicate with others. And in this case, it is not about English, Spanish or French, but about the nature of the language itself. In most all cases, it is about a language of simplicity that communicates truthfully but caringly and lovingly with others. If it is possible to co-mingle all the teachings I have experienced into one, this is about that co-mingling of the positive language of caring.

In the 1970's I had the distinct pleasure and ultimately the most important opportunity in my life, to meet up with Dr. Sidney B. Simon. Dr. Simon spoke about the "Language of Validation" and I came to know this as a simple and consistent method to speak in a caring way toward others and to not only build a relationship, but to actually help uplift and inspire others. As a 'language', it simply involves telling others what matters to you in your shared relationship. It uses words and phrases such as, "I admire…", "I appreciate…", "I celebrate…". "I love…" "I like….", and "I cherish…" to describe the positive qualities and experiences one person shares with another. It has no negative components, only positive VALIDATION of events, experiences, and shared times with others.

As a language, it bolsters the self-esteem of the receiver while it brings peace and joy to the communicator, and avoids any negative, critical components. Sid often referred to this language as like "having your ticket punched", a VALIDATION of something that you said or did or just WERE that was noticed and was recognized. My relationship with Dr. Sidney Simon may be the most important 'accident' that occurred during my whole career and it changed the way I thought and related to others for the rest of my years.

Along in that same time frame, I learned of a fellow in California teaching "Love 101" at the University of Southern California. His name was Dr. Leo Buscaglia and he taught about the language of LOVE. Leo, too, divided language used in communicating with others into two simple categories: 1) loving, caring statements that help build and nurture the relationship and 2) everything else that included negative comments, angry attitudes and grumpy dispositions. Leo often spoke in terms of "I love....", "I admire..." when he spoke of places he visited, people he contacted and events he encountered. But, Leo's language was never about critical or angry communications, only about LOVE.

During my time at UNC-Greensboro, I encountered several 'language' teachers and mentors, each of them preaching a similar message. One of my main reasons for going to Greensboro was to learn from Dr. William Purkey whose theory of counseling was based in language. He spoke of INVITING and DISINVITING statements and words, and how the INVITING words seemed to attract individuals to accept and embrace help in counseling or in relationships, while the DISINVITING statements, pushed them away. He also talked about how people INTENTIONALLY or UNINTENTIONALLY (accidentally) used this language. And, ultimately, if one chose to be INTENTIONALLY INVITING in much of their communication, positive results would follow. Intentional carried with it the characteristic of 'choosing' to use 'inviting' or caring and empathic words and phrases. He stressed that becoming 'intentional' in thinking about and carrying out our language with others, we could control the outcome in a positive manner. And while no communication always works with everyone, INVITING language did no harm in the process.

While in Greensboro, I began to know a group of individuals who shared a common language of helping others and that was 'person centered' counseling and speaking. Dr. C.H. Patterson, Dr. David Aspy and Dr. Robert R. Carkhuff followed in the footsteps of Dr. Carl Rogers using the language of 'empathic statements' to help others sort out problems. Carkhuff eventually developed a counselor response scale to rate levels of 'empathic statements' made by therapists in counseling sessions. In all cases, however, the 'language' was full of empathy, caring, respect and genuineness on the part of the communicator and the result was powerful in its impact on the relationship with clients and others. It too, was a language of love, caring and respect which seemed to be common characteristics of all the 'languages' I was beginning to learn.

Dr. Marion Franklin and Dr. William Glasser spoke of a simple division of 'language' that placed words, and communication in either HELPING or HURTING categories. Simply, words and phrases that were, again, caring and empathic would be HELPFUL in building relationships and in counseling clients to sort out problems in their lives. HURTING statements pushed others away, made them feel unheard and detracted from the relationship. Later I met Dr. Robert Webbolding who spoke the same language.

In short, I began to learn that Simon, Buscaglia, Purkey, Patterson, Aspy, Carkhuff, Franklin, Glasser, Webbolding and even a man named Assagioli, were speaking in a language from the same book. Maybe using slightly different wording and explanations, all the languages involved caring, respectful, empathic, grateful, validating and loving communications. Maybe if we all spoke in this 'language', the world could be a more loving and caring place to live. AND we might be more effective in our relationships with others around us.

How about your 'language'? Does criticism, anger, and accusation invade your communication style or language with others? Would it simply be more HELFUL if you chose to communicate in loving, caring, empathic, and validating ways with others? Does it really help to point out someone's faults and make them feel shunned and less important? Or, would you be more effective in your life and relationships to be validating, loving and caring with others? It is an interesting, and in many ways again SIMPLE choice to be "nice" rather than "naughty" in our talking and communicating with others. Give it some thought and evaluate you own words as you speak. Do they HELP or HURT? It IS a choice you can make. Choose the positive and eliminate the negative as often as you can. You might be surprised.

By the way, if you are interested, you can read more about the people mentioned above by checking out the book list for their written works.

8 - CHOOSING A RESPONSE

Here's A Quick Math Lesson: E + R = O

I'm not sure if I promised "NO MATH" in this book but just a quick little lesson shouldn't hurt that much. After all, we know that math is really important in our lives, especially Algebra! Anyway, here is a SIMPLE (remember simple is the best) equation that might help make some sense of the problems that can arise from our choices regarding how to act in regards to situations in our lives.

The equation is written: E + (+/- R) = +/- O   Seems simple enough. The letters stand for **E**vent, **R**esponse and **O**utcome. This is a "human behavior equation" and here is how it works.

EVENTS happen in our lives. Things happen to us, around us, even without our input. But things do happen. Much of the time, we have little or no control over events (except the ones we plan) in our lives and we are faced with the question: "What do we do now?" when an event occurs. So that explains the **E** part. Events happen. By the way, the **E** is neither a positive (+) or negative (-) by itself. It is what we call in math, a NEUTRAL element. Therefore, it has no valance (math term). So **EVENTS** are technically not positive or negative. They are only events.

So, what do we do now? We have the option to decide about **R,** our **RESPONSE** to the **E,** event. And we have only TWO choices (that may sound simply familiar from other places in this book). We can choose a **+ or −** (positive or negative) response to the event. In our other terms, we can choose a "helpful" or a "hurtful" response to the event. If you forgot these terms, review Chapter 4!

Now, here is the real point of the whole equation. Since the **E** is neutral, the valence of the **O** (**OUTCOME**) is directly affected by the valence of the **R** (**RESPONSE**). Maybe this is getting too technical. Simply, what this means is that outcome or result of an event in our lives is at the mercy of our response to those events in our lives. The events themselves are NOT the determining factor of our emotions. A flat tire on our vehicle doesn't really make us MAD! IT is only a flat tire – an event (not positive or negative). We produce a positive or negative outcome from that event by the way we <u>choose to behave</u> toward the flat tire.

Now, granted this may seem too simple and our emotions can be pretty strong at times. But think about it. A flat tire is a flat tire. Nothing you can do will simply make it puff up again. You can grab a knife and slash the other three tires. You can get the tire iron and break out the windows of your vehicle. And you can take the tire iron and make dents in the doors, hood and top of your vehicle. But the tire will still be flat. And your vehicle will probably look pretty rough! $E + (-R) = -O$ (This is for the math folks). That is (in words) if we respond in a NEGATIVE way toward the (Neutral) EVENT we will get, in return, a NEGATIVE Outcome. Simply math.

Again, those would be NEGATIVE responses or "hurtful" responses to the neutral event and would result in a negative outcome. But what if you chose to simply open the trunk, get out the spare and jack, remove the flat tire, replace it with the spare (or if you want, call a wrecker service) and drive on to your destination as previously planned. You might arrive a little later than you had planned but your vehicle would still be intact. $E + (+R) = +O$ (Again, for the math folks). Translated in words, a neutral event added to a positive response results in a positive outcome. In math lingo, 0 + (+1) = +1 but 0 + (-1) = -1. That is a very different outcome or result.

Simple as this may seem, it is often true that people take a neutral event and respond negatively toward or about it and produce a negative result or outcome. We could just as easily choose helpful and positive responses and move toward a much more pleasant ending.

We would often like to blame our anger, frustration, and resentment on an event (flat tire) but the real culprit in the equation is NOT the event but our response to the event. We cannot change the past but we can effectively control our current behavior and make a difference in the future.

CHOOSE WISELY when you are RESPONDING to an EVENT!

Humankind's goals in space or on earth are limited only by the power of our processing. Humanity defines itself by its ability to facilitate this processing—in ourselves and others.

Robert R. Carkhuff, The Art of Helping 1983 Human Resource Development Press, Amherst, Mass

9 - CHOOSING TO "ACT AS IF"

In working with clients, I have often proposed they make a choice to behave or act the way they wanted to feel or be, even though that might be contrary to their current behavior or feeling. If they can bring themselves to ACT AS IF they are the way they really want to be, it is possible to achieve a positive change for themselves or others. Simply, if we "act as if" we did behave or think the way that represents how we really want to be or feel, we can grow to become that way in reality. By "acting as if", a person can actually grow to feel the way they are "acting" and begin to move toward truly becoming a person with the behavior, attitude or feeling they really, really want.

In response, I have had some people say, "So you want me to PRETEND to be happy?" "But that would be dishonest" or "I'd be lying if I did that" or "I wouldn't be true to myself if I did that". This is particularly true in cases where relationships are an issue.

But this is NOT asking the person to 'pretend'. PRETENDING is actually "playing like" you are someone one or have some ability that you don't really have but with the intention of returning to your "old self" after the playing is over. It is a PRETENSE with an ENDING. Much like in a movie or play when people "play" characters they have no intention of becoming and will return to their 'normal lives' after the play or movie ends. The word PRET-END itself suggests that what you are doing is only for a short time and will END at some point.

ACTING AS IF is a conscious choice to behave or think in ways that can lead toward becoming a different person and it is a process of CHANGE. Most of us have done this at different points in our lives. As children, we might have 'pretended' to be a police officer, nurse, teacher or musician. In playing those roles, we would 'play like' we thought those individuals might act. In the end, however, we went back to being our regular self and behaving just like did before.

ACTING AS IF takes a bigger step and is about setting a goal or a desired result (to actually become a great teacher, for example) and then beginning to ACT AS IF we are that person. In the case of becoming a great teacher, individuals often copy and emulate behaviors of a model teacher or teachers, with the goal of becoming a great teacher like their model(s). It is not about being the same as the model, but it is about taking on some of the positive characteristics of the model person or persons and becoming the great teacher we set out to become.

So, ACTING AS IF is much bigger than 'pretending' in that it expects a change for the better will eventually occur if we ACT consistently in certain ways for an extended period of time. Much like an apprentice or an intern, a person chooses to act, behave or think in ways they believe are connected to that end goal or result. If you want to become a great teacher, you begin to act as if you are one by behaving in ways you consider great teachers behave. As with becoming an artist, welder, cook, or parent, by choosing to behave as if you possessed the skills, talents and knowledge needed to become such a person, you would begin to work toward doing the things needed to become such a person and moving toward a permanent change.

This does require knowledge of how the 'model' person or persons act, think and behave and also what formal training might be needed. But once we know the key elements and characteristics of our model person, and begin to act on those key elements, we will begin to move in the direction of truly becoming a similar person and growing beyond our former behavior and thinking toward becoming the person we truly want.

In the end, by ACTING AS IF, we actually become the different person we set out to become that is more like the person we really want to be. In relationships, we can do this as well by determining the characteristics of a 'great spouse', 'great lover' or 'great parent' and choosing to incorporate some of those characteristics into our daily lives and interactions with others. Once we know HOW to behave, we simply CHOOSE TO ACT AS IF that is our 'normal behavior' but with the intention of actually incorporating those behaviors into our personal behavior as a positive permanent change.

So, the big question is what are the things I need to do to become the person I really want to be? It will take some study and thought, but come up with a list of behaviors, knowledge and thoughts common to a person with that skill set, character or ability and pick the ones you can and will incorporate into your actions. And remember, this is not about "playing like", it is about ACTING AS IF you actually have those characteristics with the intention of becoming a person who DOES have those characteristics.

If we choose to "act as if" in situations that really matter personally and where we would really like to see change or improvement, could we actually see a positive change? If we choose to "act as if" our relationship is more like we really, really want it be, is there a chance it might actually begin to become more of what we really, really want? Well, the truth is YES. Often, if we "act as if" in positive ways to move toward something we want, we are able to bring about change in a situation and make it more like what we want it to be on a regular basis.

And besides, as we have said before, if what you are doing or have been doing is NOT making a situation better, it's time to choose some other way to act or think, especially a way that would help you feel better and maybe result in a better day for you and all others concerned.

EXERCISE: Write down some ways you could CHOOSE to 'act as if' in order to move in a positive direction with someone or some situation. Where would you like to see positive change? What could you DO to make that happen? What could you say? Start right here:

ACTING AS IF

- What I could do to act as if life was like I really wanted it to be:

I could..... put a smile on my face and 'act as if' I am happy more of the time.

I could..... make plans for a dinner out and invite my spouse for a 'date night'.

I could.....

I could.....

I could.....

I could.....

- What I could do to generate the positive interaction I would really like to have:

I could….. say something pleasant to the person and truly attempt to have them feel happy.

I could….. listen carefully as my spouse tells about an event in their life.

I could…..

I could…..

I could…..

I could…..

- List some things the other person might like and decide what you can do to make those happen (a relationship exercise). List as many things as you can. **See if you can get 50!**

Do simple chores without someone asking.

Bring home small gifts for no particular reason….'just thought of you'.

Drop an "I LOVE YOU" card in the MAIL for your spouse.

Send a mid-day "I LOVE YOU" text to your spouse and surprise them.

Think about the many things you might do to "Act As If" and grow your life and your relationship. There's room on the next page:

Add to YOUR LIST RIGHT HERE!

10 - CHOOSING PARTICIPATION

Change in our lives does require participation on our part. However, the outcome is directly related to our level of participation. I have come to believe that there are only three levels of participation from which to choose: CREATE, PROMOTE and ALLOW. I learned this also from Dr. Simon. Let me explain the levels and let's start with the easiest level – ALLOW.

- **ALLOW:** We can ALLOW changes to take place in our lives with very little effort. This level goes hand-in-hand with the age-old statement "Let's wait and see what happens". And, sure enough, something will happen. Something ALWAYS happens. This level requires little or no action on our part. We need not even be present for the change to happen. But things will change. Nothing never happens! The unfortunate problem with allowing for change is that we often do not get the things we want or would like in our lives. We get whatever happens; things chosen and decided upon by others without our input. But since nothing stays the same, change will happen and by allowing, we can simply sit back and watch what happens. And then accept, or complain, about the outcome.

- **PROMOTE:** If we move up a level in participation to PROMOTE, we find that we have somewhat more control over the outcome of the change. At this level, we are able to make some choices about what to do or support in our lives. While we are not in total control of the offerings, we can choose for ourselves from among the things offered and thus, have some satisfaction in getting a more suitable outcome. Examples here might be that we would choose to attend a concert, party or outing that was available or to which we were invited. Now remember, we don't do much other than choose to attend or participate but we do at least have some control over what will happen and have the chance to get something closer to what we really want. Promoting requires that we at least make some effort to choose from among several alternatives and to pick something that will happen (a change) that we might like more than others, although others do most of the work.

- **CREATE:** Now to the highest level of participation: CREATE. At this level, the person is in charge of making the change or event happen. The design, planning, organization and execution of the event are in the hands of the person making the change. This, of course, is more work than the other two levels but the chances here of really getting what you REALLY want in your life have increased dramatically. The person gets to design exactly what they want to have happen and make it work. Along with this responsibility is increased risk since the success or failure of the event is based on the person's level of effort and creativity. But, the rewards are also greater since the likelihood of getting what you really want is increased.

So, it is up to you. You can:

1) wait and see what happens;

2) check out what is happening and pick one to join; or

3) create your own set of plans to guarantee you get exactly what you want.

The effort involved on your part increases with the responsibility level but the outcome moves closer to what you really, really want. If you REALLY want something or if you simply do not what others to be choosing for you, then step up to the plate and make a plan. Do what you say you are going to do and take charge. Choose wisely.

> *If you want to change attitudes, start with a change in behavior.*
>
> William Glasser

11 - CHOOSING POSITIVE THINKING

Sometimes it is easy to get "stuck" thinking in negative ways and about negative things. Sometimes, we are hurt by someone, shunned or ignored or just feel "left out" from the crowd. It is easy to fall into a poor me or pity-party mode and begin thinking about all the negative things that have happened. In fact, it is almost 'normal' for us to do that by default.

If you find yourself in that situation, here is a simple exercise you can do to switch yourself into a positive thinking mode and begin to instantly feel better about yourself and your situation. As with many things however, the key is that you choose to do this - no matter what - so it can work.

EXERCISE:

YOUR TASK: Sometime during the day, write down three (3) positive ("good") things that occurred on or during that day. You could even do these individually as they happen or all at once in the evening, but you are to get at least three things on your list. Once you have made your list of three positive things, your task is to write down three things you did to make that event or thing happen. How did YOU control YOUR behavior to CREATE that event?

This sounds simple but let's looks at an example. Let's say you were feeling lonely and isolated one day and began thinking how sad it was that people have ignored you and never spent any time with you or being your friend. But, you decided to CONTROL YOUR BEHAVIOR and "phone a friend" in an effort to re-connect with someone. As luck would have it, that friend was feeling a little isolated and alone as well and the two of you decided to meet for lunch and a little visit. So, you cleaned up and got ready to head out for lunch, met your old friend, caught up on each other's lives and work and family, and had a wonderful visit and lunch. It was so good, in fact, you decided between the two of you to meet about once a month just to visit and keep in touch. As an added benefit, both of you thought you might sometimes bring along another friend in need of company and make it even more enjoyable.

So, here is how your LIST is beginning to look:

POSITIVE EVENT #1

    1. Had a wonderful lunch and visit with a dear friend I had not seen in a while.

        a. Went through list of people I know and found someone I thought might be a good candidate for a re-connect (found several and picked one to call).
        b. Made the phone call and found that they were interested in meeting for lunch and made plans to have lunch.
        c. Dressed for lunch and met my friend having a wonderful conversation and lunch with plans to make this a regular meeting with the possibility of meeting others.

POSITIVE EVENT #2

    2. YOU FILL IN THIS ONE:
        a.
        b.
        c.

Now, how hard is that? Well, as with many things, it seems simple. It is just not easy to STOP the negative bleed and turn around to do something more positive. BUT you can do it and if you have three of these POSITIVE EVENTS each day with three behaviors you used to make each happen, at the end of the week you have twenty-one (21) positive events and sixty-three (63) positive behaviors that made a something good happen in your life.

You do the math for a month or a year if you are into math but you probably get the point. This kind of activity, simple as it is, will grow exponentially to squeeze out the negative thinking and fill your day with positive thinking about how to gain more control over what happens to you based on how you think, act and behave. And, you don't have to do three things every day forever, but you could continue doing some as often as you need them to keep on a positive track and feeling good.

"Don't put the key to your happiness in someone else's pocket - keep it in your own."

12 - CHOOSING TRUTH

Choosing to be truthful or honest with people is sometimes difficult and even more so when you are on the receiving end of the conversation. Sometimes the words "truth" and "honesty" are used interchangeably and I have used them that way as well. But here I want to make sure there is a clear distinction to be considered when we are faced with telling the truth. If you hear someone say, "Let me be perfectly honest with you", my advice is the RUN, grab up your things and GET OUT OF THERE! That person is about to unload a pile of junk on you that you probably already know about and rub it in so that you end up feeling miserable and hurt. The word "perfectly" seems to change the dimension whether it is used in combination with honest or truthful. Perfectly honest or perfectly truthful is often aimed at making someone feel bad and also may contain a lot of the communicator's own problem issues.

So let's think about it this way. It is important to be truthful. If you are truthful, you won't have to try to remember what you told others since it will always be the same thing! I used to tell my middle school students that in counseling since they would often have several versions of the real truth before they would actually 'lie' about something. Their problem was that they would forget who they told what and after a while, it was a pretty big mess.

Truth is about fact. Truth is about helping someone understand or know something. But it is also about saying "I will tell you the truth and then if you have any questions, I will answer them as truthfully as I can". It is not intended to hurt anyone, just to provide essential information needed to understand or make a decision about something.

In counseling and in teaching about counseling, I often used and taught about "therapeutic truthfulness". In my mind, that is about telling the truth, but not necessarily the "whole truth and nothing but the truth" since some information, while it may be the 'truth' is really not necessary for the other person to have in order to understand and resolve an issue. "Therapeutic Truthfulness" is about telling the necessary elements of a group of facts or information about an event but understanding that it is alright (and it is not LYING) to leave out some of the unessential elements that are 'true' but do not really contribute to understanding and resolution.

Here is a situation that might help explain. Over my years of counseling and helping, I have often dealt with grief and death situations. In these situations, there are facts that are truthful and are helpful in resolving and coming to grips with such an event. There are also facts that, while they may be truthful, are unnecessary, and may even be harmful to the resolution.

One situation that comes to mind is in dealing with a young child about the death of a parent. In truth, the parent was murdered by a gang. That's the TRUTH. But will that help a young child resolve the loss of a parent? Chances are that truthful information will only establish a deeper set of problems in the child's brain and will not help at all, in fact, make things worse. So, therapeutically, is that information necessary to help the child to resolve the loss? I don't think so. You can decide, but for me, the death is enough to work with in therapy and the method of dying may not be at all helpful to the child. Remember now, it IS the truth, but will it help for the child to know and attempt to process that truth in working toward resolution. Later in life, there might be information the child, as an older teen or adult, may want to know, but maybe not. If they want to know more, they can ask. You have not lied about the death, only left out brutal details that would have most likely added to the suffering and loss. And, by the way, children often know much more than we give them credit for knowing!

I could share other such examples but you probably get the picture. Some truth just is not important to helping solve a problem and can be 'selected out' of the discussion. By doing this, we do what I like to think of a "rounding the sharp corners of truth" and keep the truth from cutting and hurting so much. It is still the truth, but the blow of the truth is softened.

We can "round the sharp corners" many times when we are being truthful and attempting to help people resolve issues without using the "brutally honest" words sometimes used by others. You can decide on this one and how you want to respond. I recommend you choose 'therapeutic truthfulness". You decide.

"If you tell the truth, you don't have to remember anything."
— Mark Twain

I loved to quote this passage to my students in middle school. They would often tell something a dozen different ways before they would lie about it! And they would get into the most trouble trying to remember which version they told which of their friends!

13 - CHOOSING PATIENCE

Being patient is often such a struggle for people. We are always in such a rush to get somewhere or to finish something. As parents, we are impatient with our children and fail to take a few extra minutes to allow them an opportunity to do something new or challenging to them. We act in angry ways toward those who seem to go 'too slow' in the checkout line in the grocery store or people who 'can't go fast enough' on a small road when we can't pass them up and get on with our travel.

PATIENCE is a virtue, I have heard said. I know that in my counseling efforts, PATIENCE is essential when we allow a client to think through a problem, knowing that WE KNOW the answer. But it is important to just patiently "be there" with the client while they struggle through a difficult moment and search for THEIR answer to THEIR problem. After all, OUR answer to THEIR problem will probably not be worth much to them in the long run. We, as counselors, need to save OUR answers for OUR problems since we have them as well.

"Psychotherapy is about *being with,* not *doing something to,* the client", my mentor and teacher Dr. C.H. Patterson would say so often. And he was the embodiment of that concept. Having learned and studied with Dr. Carl Rogers, he 'preached' Rogers' theory which was very clear about listening more than talking. It was about hearing what the client had to say and helping them to hear their own answers. It was NOT about pumping in outside information.

It seems that sometimes, in today's world of counseling and therapy, professionals push to have a set of correct answers or a series of specific steps that a person would take to solve their problem. "Too many counselors operate on the assumption that there are general answers to problems which must be given to the client, or to which the client must be subtly led. But there are no general answers - there are only specific ones for each client, which the client must find for her/himself. "(C.H. Patterson) And if we have PATIENCE, each client will eventually find the answers they seek. Some take longer than others and some problems will be more difficult to answer than others but the answers will always be within the person who is seeking assistance.

An old Chinese proverb stated that when the young student asked his Master, "Master, where should I go to find the path to happiness?" and the Master's reply was, "Oh my son, there is NO path to happiness. Happiness lives within the person who walks upon the path."

PATIENCE allows us the time to seek out our own answers and our own path. CHOOSE PATIENCE with yourself AND with others and you will maximize your relationship and your own personal growth.

Patience is waiting. Not passively waiting. That is laziness. But to keep going when the going is hard and slow - that is patience. The two most powerful warriors are patience and time. **Leo Tolstoy**

14 - CHOOSING FAITH

Faith sustains people in many situations that might often seem unbearable. Relying on FAITH on a daily basis gives one the assurance that, at some point, everything will work out and life will be good. My Mom had a tremendous faith in everything being alright and working out for the best. So many times, I have heard her say, "just have faith and things will work out". In my early years as a teenager, I was called on to speak at church during Youth Sunday. I remember thinking about what would I say and do in front of all those people in the church where I had grown up. People who knew me my whole life and at that point, probably knew me better than I knew myself.

But the answer to my dilemma came pretty quickly when I thought about my Mom and her faith. "If you have faith, even as little as a mustard seed, nothing will be impossible to you." So that was it. I even had a children's version with small cards and mustard seed glued on the card to show them just how small an amount that would be. Mustard seeds are small! And that was all it would take, if you just had that much faith.

I am not sure just how my Mom was able to stand by her faith sometimes. She had hard times, especially after the death of my Father when I was only six. And she never looked back. Never considered NOT going on alone and set her sights on making things work out for the best. I know it took a tremendous leap of faith for her to allow me to drive off when I got my license at age 16 in a car that I had built from scratch when I was 15. Just allowing me to take that risk itself was a challenge. But she was, as I have said, one of the strongest people I have ever known. She never lost FAITH and she taught me to do the same.

FAITH allows us to free ourselves from worry, to let go of jealousy, and to believe in the goodwill of others. It bolsters our relationships when we believe and have faith that the other person will do right by us and that everything will work out for the benefit of all.

"It is not necessary to see in order to believe…must you see the WIND to know that it is there?" Chinese Proverb

Faith is to believe what you do not see; the reward of this faith is to see what you believe.   **Saint Augustine**

*"If you have faith as a **mustard seed**, you will **say** to this mountain, move from here to there, and it will move; and nothing will be **impossible** for you".* Matthew 17:20 and Luke 17:6.

15 - CHOOSING RESPECT & COURTESY

RESPECT was more than just a song back in the mid-1950s, it was a VALUE that people grew up learning and acting upon. Along with some other 'old timey values', RESPECT has faded considerably and is often non-existent in some people's lives and existence. As a counselor, I have witnessed so many cases where the simple omission of respectful behaviors and words accounted for the majority of problems.

Maybe it is about not being taught respectful behavior? And I am sure it is about not being treated respectfully by others. I am reminded of the old statement, "Be respectful to your elders!". I heard that said many times and those were not casual words: they were meant to be HEARD and DONE!

CHOOSING is what this book is all about and here is another option where YOU can CHOOSE to be RESPECTFUL and COURTEOUS. Or not. But it is a CHOICE. In my work with children, couples and families for almost 50 years now, I have seen how simple RESPECT can strengthen and improve any relationship when it is present.

I worked throughout my career with teenagers and often talked with them about the 'qualities' they might want to have in a relationship or their own family. The young women often got this one pretty early and they were clear about it as well. They saw RESPECT and COURTESY as key elements to any relationship and always ranked that higher than 'money', 'popular' or 'handsome'. They wanted someone who was COURTEOUS and who would be RESPECTFUL to them. Sometimes the guys would get it too but usually later on.

The ladies had it right. Being respectful and courteous wins you points with others. It's that simple. And it is a choice, today more than ever. Think of it as courteous behavior, on the highway, in the grocery store, wherever you find yourself in a situation where you can 'give someone else a break'. Treat someone with respect and courtesy when you get a chance. It is a gift you give yourself since it will make you feel good in return!

ASSIGNMENT:

1. If you are in a line for something, anything, and you notice someone who is older or having difficulty with waiting, invite them to go ahead of you (be careful not to put them ahead of someone else only you!).
2. A really fun thing is to "pick up the tab" for someone you don't know at a restaurant. Just simply tell the cashier that you want to pay for that person's meal, and leave. When they get ready to pay, imagine their surprise.
3. And you can always offer to open or hold a door for someone, it's an old one, but it is still COURTEOUS.
4. Find ways to TEACH RESPECT and COURTESY to your children and others. You will be glad you did and so will they!
5. NOW, think of some other ways you can be courteous and respectful with others. Be sure to do them sometimes. Start your list here and do these things - maybe even often.

No act of kindness,
no matter how small,
is ever wasted.

- Aesop

16 - CHOOSING RESPONSIBILITY

Choosing to BE RESPONSIBLE is probably at the core of this entire book. It is about BEING RESPONSIBLE by CHOICE to CONTROL your life so that it works for your benefit, as well as the benefit of others. It is about DOING what you promise to do and following through with anything you begin.

RESPONSIBILITY is something I have seen erode over the years as I have grown into adulthood. I have spent my professional career working with individuals who, in many cases, have lost the vision of 'being responsible' for their own behavior and thinking and failing to teach or pass along the concept of "responsibility" to their children. In many cases, their parents failed (or simply did not know themselves) to be responsible. This erosion has been occurring for several decades as some of you reading this may have seen the loss as well.

I remember being taught as a child, early on, to BE RESPONSIBLE for your behavior, your clothing, your toys and your words. Irresponsible behavior was simply not tolerated much that I can remember. If you left your ball glove outside and it rained, your glove got soaked with water and then the leather became hard, cracked and you had to spend hours with saddle soap attempting to get the leather soft enough to work again as a ball glove. The same thing happened with your bicycle, clothing, and other possessions. As children, at an early age, I remember being 'required' to be responsible for our own 'stuff'.

We also learned about being responsible toward other people, items that belonged to others and taking care of our own mess. It was not a bad thing to learn. It was about BEING RESPONSIBLE. At first, we didn't get to "choose" but later on, as we had been required to do, we began to choose to be responsible and to be known as a 'responsible person'. That's a nice character trait and one that is sometimes missing now some 50 years later.

Unfortunately, over the decades, 'being responsible' has faded and is often difficult to find in some people today. However, here's where your CHOICE becomes essential. If you know that choosing to be responsible for your day-to-day actions and thoughts is within your control, then, you can simply CHOOSE RESPONSIBLE behavior.

You can also choose to TEACH RESPONSIBLE behavior to children, family and yes, even adults around you. By CHOOSING RESPONSIBILITY, you can model what RESPONSIBILITY looks like, just like it was modeled for some of us back in the day when it was the popular thing to do. We saw it happing on a regular basis, and we copied what we saw happening. We were expected to do as we SAW DONE! Not just as we were told to do but as we were SHOWN how to do. We even saw responsible behavior on television, when we were allowed to watch television.

It is a good concept, RESPONSIBILITY, and one which needs to taken more seriously and brought back into popularity today.

17 - CHOOSING NEGOTIATION and FAIRNESS

Sometimes we confuse 'fair' with 'equal' and there is a struggle to match up everything "dollar for dollar" to be FAIR to ALL. If we attempt to be EQUAL with everything, we will spend a lot of time counting the numbers, time, days, or dollars each person gets so that everything will be EQUAL.

So, instead, let us consider what FAIR means. Being FAIR is simply making sure that everyone involved in a situation or event walks away feeling that they were treated with respect and a sense of being satisfied with the result. It is NOT about exact numbers but it is about feeling satisfied and 'happy' with the result.

Often in families, I hear the argument that "it's your night to do the dishes, I did them last night!", or "why is it that I always have to take out the trash?". In working with others, we are often faced with how to level the playing field and have the entire group involved in a decision. Everyone could feel as though they were treated fairly, NOT EQUALLY necessarily, but FAIRLY. And, in the end, they would all be satisfied with the result.

Now, this is not an easy task but there is one simple rule I learned in a marriage and family class while I was in Greensboro. The professor said, "I only have one rule for marriages and that is that EVERYTHING is NEGOTIABLE, *except* NEGOTIATION." That stuck with me and I have often used that concept in working with families over the years.

While we cannot be exactly 'equal' in every way with everything, we can NEGOTIATE a fair settlement with most everything we do and especially in families. Negotiation means that each one involved will have a say in what might be considered 'fair' to them. As each person is heard in the negotiation, everyone's thoughts and needs are considered.

In NEGOTIATION, there is none of the WIN-LOSE game playing. Negotiation is about WIN-WIN and in the final analysis, each person feels as if their concerns and needs were at least considered and they were able to get some of what they wanted in the final DEAL. In negotiation, no one gets all of what they want. It is part of the deal to have GIVE and TAKE and each person in the negotiation wins some and loses some but comes out winning enough to feel satisfied.

Families with several members (children, mom, dad) who use NEGOTIATION to solve daily problems in and around the home and in other areas of living, find that everyone is more content with the total outcome and everyone 'wins' enough be to happy.

Give this one a spin. Next time you and some others (family, co-workers, etc.) are involved in a problem that appears to be a WIN-LOSE situation, see if you can move toward negotiating a solution where everyone will walk away satisfied. It really is not as hard as arguing and fighting and the end result is much more pleasant.

18 - CHOOSING "FORGIVENESS"

FORGIVENESS. It seems like a very hard thing to do, but if we can do it, it can be a major key to our future happiness. What makes it difficult for most of us to do is in the way it has been defined for us by our teachers (parents and friends). We think of forgiveness as meaning that we should say EVERYTHING is "forgotten", ALL is "OK", and we will just simply put it out of our mind or memory and life will be just like it was before the hurt. We have all heard "let by-gone's, be by-gone's" theory, but that is not really possible.

Our brain simply is not set up to 'forget'. The fact is, that if we 'forgot' things that easily, we would keep making the same bad mistakes over and over. So we DO remember. And we even remember BAD things. That is true so we won't allow or do them again! PLUS, we remember the good things we did and things that worked well for us so that we can REPEAT those good things. So, we don't want to wish 'forgetting' as a widespread gift to everyone.

To enjoy the personal benefits of forgiveness all we really have to do is make the decision to move forward and let go of the old hurt. We don't have to condone what's been done. What was wrong is still wrong. We don't have to invite the person back into our lives or even be friendly with them. We don't have to say 'it's OK' or 'don't worry about it' like we sometimes hear said. People usually don't really mean that anyway. They are just 'being nice'. We can even express some anger about what happened and that's alright too.

To accomplish FORGIVENESS, we simply need to allow ourselves to release the negative emotions associated with that person and/or event. As long as we hold onto the pain, we are choosing to allow those past actions to continue to hurt us. We can CHOOSE to stop allowing them hurt us. We can CHOOSE to focus on our future and on the positive things happening NOW in our lives. That makes forgiveness a little more possible for most of us and will allow us to move on through the past hurt and get on with our future and our life. We can say 'good-bye' to the hurt and leave it sitting by the road. Forgiveness actually frees up the 'forgiver' more than anyone.

Generally speaking our brain WON'T ever 'forget' what happened, but we can choose to put it off to the side, unhook ourselves from it and move forward. In fact, we really need to remember what happened so it doesn't have a chance of hurting us again in the future. But, we can 'stop the bleed' as some medical people might say. And, while we may always have a 'scar' from the hurt, we don't have to keep suffering from the pain.

"In Forgiveness, we come to understand: that the ability to forgive is not a sign of weakness but of profound emotional strength; that in order to forgive we do not need to forget and, perhaps more important; that, through the process of forgiving others, the only person we are 'letting off the hook', is our self." Sidney B. Simon/Suzanne Simon, FORGIVENESS, 1990, Warner Books, NY

Without forgiveness life is governed by...
an endless cycle of resentment and retaliation.
- Roberto Assagioli

Choosing to Forgive . . .

Unlocks the Cell to the Prison inside your
heart – it sets YOU free!

19 - CHOOSING TALKING and WRITING

At least sometimes, choose to TALK to your spouse, family, friends and others and MAYBE even HAND WRITE a card or letter to them and drop it in the 'snail mail'. I am not against technology and in fact, have applauded the advances I have enjoyed over my life. However, I have not forgotten that sometimes it is the spoken word and the hand written message that means so much and makes so much difference in a communication.

I was recently reminded how much I too depend on technology (especially cell phone) to communicate with others. When I went to check my phone messages early one morning, my phone was blinking green but would not turn on or off. No matter what I tried to do, it just 'laughed at me in green' as to say it was on break or still taking a nap. Ultimately, I learned another trick to gain control but not after some panicky moments thinking about all the phone numbers, messages, etc. that I would not be able to get back. You know the feeling I am sure.

When we choose to talk out loud to someone, we communicate more than fact, word or texted message. We actually communicate our FEELINGS about what we are saying. Having been a counselor and professor for almost fifty years, I could not begin to think about doing much with 'long distance' counseling over the phone or teaching classes 'on-line' that had to do with counseling technique and responding to clients. As well as, being able to determine more about the "real meaning" of the clients words. Without being able to SEE and HEAR the unspoken elements of the conversation, I felt I would be at a terrible disadvantage.

Some of my most cherished memories include hand written cards and notes or letters from my Mom or my wife (when we were dating) and from colleagues like Sid Simon and Leo Buscaglia who typed letters but used a manual typewriter and small note paper and always signed their name in ink. Such a lasting gift those cards, letters and even recordings that I play over and over even today. We do still have video and that is a good thing.

I encourage each of you to sit down with your older relatives, make a point to do this, and record them talking with you and telling you about their life and about your other family. Someday, you will wish you had done this, so, just do it now or as soon as you possibly can before it's too late. I used this as an assignment is some of my classes as a project and students who chose to do it came by years later and thanked me for making that an assignment. Now they have a record of that person who is no longer living but can speak to them in picture and word through a recorded interview.

Choosing to talk and write are sometimes difficult in today's world. We are busy, separated and unavailable to others but there are SOME times that we could choose to write and talk out loud. While I was working on this book, I called Robert "Bob" Carkhuff's publishing company where I had visited some 35-40 years before and spoke with a wonderfully inviting young woman who answered the phone. I asked if Bob was around and she said he was not but after I told her the reason for my call and that I wanted to say 'Hello' again, she asked me to leave my number and she would have Bob call me back. I went on about my business for the day, but happened to be home for a little while and the phone rang. I answered and the voice on the other end asked, "Hello, is the Steve?". I thought; who could this be? I had left my cell phone for "Bob" to call so it couldn't be him. But, before I could say much, he said, "HI, this is Bob Carkhuff" returning your call.

As it turned out, this was Bob's SON, who had been quite young when I was at "The MILL" in Amherst, Massachusetts. But, nonetheless, young Bob had taken the time to track down my home phone number and call back. It meant so much to know he would be that concerned. We exchanged some conversation and I learned some about his dad, the Bob I knew, who was still well and he agreed to pass along my words to his Dad. We did exchange email addresses and I later sent an email just to follow-up but the sound of a voice and the effort to make a phone call, was more special than I even thought it would be.

Later in that same day, I called up my good friend and mentor, Dr. Sidney Simon for a '5-minute love call' to say hello and catch up on when we might see each other. And maybe talk about writing some more on a book, or cooking some fish on the grill or going to see a play or concert. We laughed and chatted but it was REAL. Real talking, word of mouth, hearing and speaking, hearing the tone and the inflection. It was BETTER THAN TEXT!!!

Here are your assignments:

 1. Videotape/record an interview with some of your older relatives as soon as you can and ask them all the questions you need to have answered about family, their lives as a kid, and about what they remember of you as a kid, everything you need to know. (Maybe you could do SEVERAL!)

2. Make a list of several people with whom you need to TALK more on a regular basis and be sure you have their phone numbers. THEN, pick one or two for the next couple days and

make a phone call to say "Hello" and talk over old times. Better yet, sit down with them and have a REAL conversation in person. I am also thinking about married couples here and parents with their children. Do it before it's too late.

3. Take that same list and maybe add a name or two and get out a pen and stationery or cards and start writing a message, short is fine, to several of the folks on that list. You can also send newspaper clippings of things that might be of interest to them, pictures of your family, articles you have read, great recipes, anything that you think would be nice to send, and then mail it off to them. Be sure to sign your letter, and yes, if you don't like to write a lot you can type it on the computer, print it out BUT you need to SIGN IT IN INK!... In your own handwriting, and maybe add a little hand-written note about something. It will be a treasure to them I am sure.

OK, that's enough about talking and writing. But remember, there is NEVER enough of that these days; we have way too much technology to balance that out so get busy writing and talking!

Leave your love ones a handwritten note today!!!

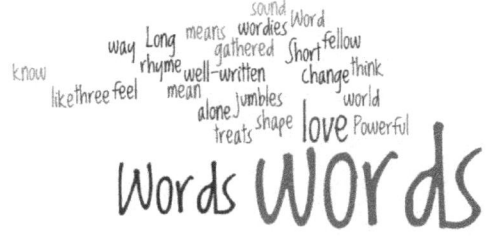

20 - CHOOSING DAILY ACHIEVEMENTS

The terms one-a-day, or one day at a time have been used for many years in many ways. We won't go into that here but hope to think of this as a way to make a commitment toward a positive behavior that, if you accomplish this task each day, you will begin to feel more positive about yourself and more successful in your life and work.

I learned this technique from a friend who is a photographer. It so happens that she shared her "New Year's Resolution" of making at least ONE great photograph each day of the New Year. Now, to some that seems simple, but we are talking here about really great photographs, with special effects, multiple layers, composite groupings – REALLY good, really special works of art.

As I thought about that concept, it led me to expand that to a general one-a-day commitment for moving toward a successful week, month and year for anyone. It is about choosing to do something that is special – "GREAT", each day. ONLY ONE THING but a GREAT THING. Obviously, this would amount to some 365 "Great Things" at the end of a year (maybe 366 on leap year!).

WHAT IF you chose something you like or want to do such as writing, woodworking, photography, music, painting, gardening, sewing, teaching, etc. and plan to do ONE significantly great thing each day in terms of that activity. Be it a great photo, a new poem or story, a piece of art, a planting, or a lesson plan, by the end of the month, you would have some 28-31 GREAT additions to your life activity. Of course, after a year, if math serves us correctly, you would have 365 or more, GREAT productions from your efforts.

So what's the point? The point is that when we ACHIEVE and produce these great works we feel better about our self. Achieving and accomplishing builds our "self-esteem". And, what about that book you wanted to write or special garden you wanted to have? After several months, that project would begin to shape up and soon develop into a full reality, one day at a time, one great thing (step) at a time. Getting started is often a major stumbling block for individuals in moving toward a special goal.

This exercise is about "just one". Do just ONE THING each day that adds to that greater goal of a book, a garden, a better teaching plan, a personal art portfolio – whatever your goal. It will make it seem so much more possible doing it "one-day-at-a-time", one great piece at a time.   Check it out for yourself. What is it you have always wanted to do but never had the time? Pick that goal and decide what you can do once a day to make that happen. Break larger projects into small steps that can be accomplished in a shorter time. Then, add the steps together and the finished project begins to emerge.

I think I am feeling better already since this book is one of my goals and this is another chapter for that book. I hope it has made a positive impact on your life goal. It is how I got back to writing this book: 1 hour/day x 7 days/week. Pick your goal and get started! One day, one great thing at a time.

YOU COULD START A "TO DO LIST" RIGHT HERE!

21 - CHOOSING SELF-EVALUATION

As a teacher educator and supervisor for student teachers, Maymie Porter developed a simple but powerful model to use in evaluating student teachers and helping them to grow and become even better teachers. Her method is unique in that it does not call attention to or emphasize their weaknesses or punish their shortcomings. We have seen usefulness in this model as a supervision tool in other settings and also in cases of individual growth and change.

The beauty of the concept is that not only does it work for the current event, but also teaches the person a method of self-evaluating for future behavior and situations. Let me explain this simple model. It involves asking yourself [or someone] three questions and then stepping back to clearly listen to each answer and allow yourself or others to discover their own answers.

QUESTION ONE: "What do I [you] like about what I [you are] am currently doing in this situation?"

Interestingly, the theory starts out emphasizing what we LIKE about our behavior. This is contrary to what we might normally think of in 'evaluations' where often our failures are the focus, This model assumes that recognizing 'likes' or successful behaviors is really more important to increasing success rate in future efforts, What we know as well is that focusing on failures is damaging to self esteem. Conversely, focusing on the successful elements tends to build or reinforce self-image.

QUESTION TWO: "What would I [you] do differently now that I [you] know more/different information about the situation and that, if I did that, it might work more effectively?"

Once again, typical criticism is avoided by treating what we disliked about out effort as a chance to learn what did not work well in that situation. Taking what we did and modifying it in some way that might be more successful if we faced a similar situation in the future is probably more sensible than simply pointing out what was 'wrong'.

QUESTION THREE: "What help or resources do I [you] need to make this change really work?"

Finally, in an effort to put our learning into action, we are asked to consider information, data, experience or support we could use or might need to learn to help increase future success.

Behind Maymie's theory is the idea that most people: 1] know when they make a mistake; 2] know what they need to do to 'fix' the mistake; and 3] have experienced enough punishment in the past such that additional punishment or criticism will likely be ineffective and even harmful. The central idea is to eliminate punishment and guide the individual to **self-evaluate** and develop a personal plan for change. Not a bad concept to carry with us on a day-to-day basis.

MY SELF-EVALUATION IF I DID IT TODAY - RIGHT NOW

Use the THREE QUESTIONS ABOVE and answer honestly!

22 - CHOOSING TO MEET MY NEEDS

As I have said before, much of managing our lives and growing healthy can be pretty simple. Here are three simple words that can mean everything to our healthy mental and physical wellbeing. To be completely 'healthy', we need to consider each of these three areas: Physical, Mental and Spiritual. The tough part is that we don't have a 'test' or a 'meter' to check if we are "low" on something so we have to stay tuned in to our own body to know when we need to check the balance or up the level.

PHYSICAL: Let's start with the PHYSICAL first and consider how we can 'choose' to meet that need in our lives. Many people talk about 'getting more exercise' but how many of us actually DO something to make that happen? There are some very simple choices we can make that will put that in place easily and without really changing much of what we do. "Getting more exercise" is sometimes as simple as taking the stairs rather than the elevator at work, church or school. If that is possible and you are able to walk up stairs, simply CHOOSE the stairs as often as you can and that alone will HELP in your physical well-being. Granted, some individuals need the elevator because of handicapping conditions or carrying large loads, so the stair option does not apply to you if that is your situation. But, if you can, CHOOSE THE STAIRS.

Other options for simple daily choices are to park your car a little farther away from the front of the office or store and walk just a little more to get to and from your car. Secondly, form a walking club at work, school or in your neighborhood and establish a time each week (or times) to walk at lunch, or after work, or whenever the group decides. Rather than watch television, TAKE A WALK! Another option is to simply "COUNT CARBS" in your diet and watch what (and how much) you eat. You don't have to give up bread, potatoes, etc., but it does help if you watch how much you eat and how often you eat them. Have healthy snacks (not a bag of chips or cookies!) and increase your intake of protein. You might be surprised just how much you can enjoy eating healthy AND you will enjoy feeling better and losing some of the extra pounds you want to shed. Other ideas are running, biking and swimming groups or clubs and joining a health club or YMCA to have access to weight machines, treadmills, and other health programs. If you are of certain ages (senior especially), there may be FREE or reduced rates for many of these organizations. While this might require a change in schedule, it might be worth the change. CHOOSE PHYSICAL HEALTH and you are one-third of the way home on this challenge.

MENTAL: Choosing to meet mental health needs may be just as simple as "taking the stairs" seems to physical health. Here are some thoughts about how to CHOOSE MENTAL HEALTH options. If you are an avid television watcher but find yourself 'flipping channels' to find something you are willing to watch that you don't really like but it will serve to 'fill the time', turn OFF the TV! Replace some of the TV TIME with reading a good book (if you like to read), working crossword or Sudoku puzzles, (keep a puzzle book near your favorite chair) or playing some board games with your spouse and/or children. By the way, the children NEED this too! Avoid getting on the computer to immerse yourself in social media, texting, surfing or otherwise staring at the computer screen. One minor exception might be if you play solitaire or Sudoku on the computer but that is ONLY ONE and you still might be better off with a nice printed puzzle book and give your eyes a rest from the computer screen.

Other MENTAL health alternatives are choosing to have lunch with a group of friends every week on a certain day, or an evening meal out each week to enjoy some fun and laughter with your family and others. If you are able to schedule time each week, make sure you have a good full hour plus some travel time to make this work. You might even take up writing some if you enjoy writing, or drawing, painting or other craft project work. There is always the option to check out the offerings at the local community college or home extension agent office and sign up for a class to learn about something you have always liked or wanted to do (but never had the time!). Having a garden in the summer (or year-round for some things), doing your own yard work (works for PHYSICAL too) and having friends over for a dinner party or cookout can all be fun and more mentally uplifting, as well as physically in some cases, than watching TV and sitting home alone. Being productive at something whether it is learning a new skill, canning or freezing your own 'homegrown' fruits and vegetables, or spending some fun, relaxing time with friends and family are all great ways to choose MENTAL health for your life.

SPIRITUAL: The third area of need may be the most important in many ways, but may also be the most ignored or malnourished of the three areas of need. Feeding our SPIRITUAL self does not necessarily mean going to church every time the doors are open. It DOES mean, however, that we DO some things on a regular basis to focus on building and feeding our SPIRITUAL self. Certainly, going to a church of your choice is a great way to regularly feed this area of need. Many people set aside a day or more to attend church services and worship with family and friends each week. This is exceptionally important and is somewhat 'easy' in that the church sets up a planned time and program that one has only to attend to be positively impacted. So that makes this an easy and powerful ways to feed the SPIRITUAL need area.

So what else is available? Many times there are non-denominational groups that meet for support and spiritual uplifting. Reading devotional materials designed to be spiritually thoughtful is another option. Prayer, meditation and singing are also options chosen by many individuals to uplift their spiritual well-being. Individuals who enjoy music can form singing groups or 'bands' to gather on a regular basis to 'make a joyful noise' and build spiritual well-being. Choosing actions and thoughts in the SPIRITUAL area is clearly one of more individual preference BUT the need to feed the SPIRITUAL self is critical. CHOOSE OPENLY.

MAKE A LIST HERE OF THINGS YOU CAN AND WOULD LIKE TO DO TO MEET SOME OF YOUR OWN NEEDS WHILE YOU ARE THINKING OF THEM!

23 - CHOOSING A SUPPORT GROUP

A vitally important part maintaining a healthy emotional self and life depends on having a simple but effective support group around us at all times. These individuals need not be present all at once and not even all the time, but need to be available to us as we need support. Some of us get by very well on our extended family but in recent years it has become increasingly difficult to maintain family close by enough to be helpful.

There are FOUR specific individual characters we need to make up the group and they are described as follows:

- INTELLECTUAL

    This person, as a member of our support group or network, provides material and stimulation for learning, growing, becoming and developing as a person. Intellectuals often share important books to read, information on various activities or events that would be of academic nature, and maybe even teach us some skill or concept applicable to our lives.

- CONFIDANTE

    The CONFIDANTE, is a non-judgmental listener that makes us feel really 'heard' when we need a person to talk with and will never use our personal thoughts, words or shared problems to hurt us. They are a 'safe' place to communicate our most confusing and painful thoughts without worry.

- HUMOR, FUN & ADVENTURE

  In this case, as it sounds from the name, we need someone in our group who is fun to be around, is care-free and rejuvenating in words and activities that bring us fun and enjoyment and help us to recharge our emotional batteries. These people are interested in having a good time and taking you with them on the ride.

- CHICKEN SOUP

  We also need a loving, caring, comforting and healing person available to us in difficult times of need when we feel weak and helpless. This person will have what it takes to bring us back on line and feel better, all-be-it 'chicken soup' for real or other ways to be caring and nurturing to us when we need it. My Mom was a "chicken soup" person

So, now the question is WHO are these people in your life? Are you missing in any area? And what one of these roles are you often asked to portray in someone else's life? We all need support at times, most of the time, and need at least to know that it is available if and when we need it. CHOOSE these people wisely and be willing to BE CHOSEN yourself as other's need this support as well.

EXERCISE: In the following space, write down individuals you now have or you think might qualify a good support group members. Make note of the "area" they service in your support group and it might be good to have a couple for each area.

Also, write down a list of people to whom you believe YOU are a support person and what area you might service in their lives. In this case, you could provide different support for different individuals. This is an important list to have and if you are lacking in one or more areas, do some serious thinking about who might fill up that list and consider giving them a call to see if they would be willing. You can also offer yourself to individuals who seem to need support but they may be reluctant to ask. You can offer to join them for lunch or just talk on the phone. But chances are, everyone out there is lacking in one or more of the FOUR areas.

HERE IS A SPACE TO MAKE YOUR LIST:

WHO ARE YOUR SUPPORT PEOPLE?

AREAS of SUPPORT:

- INTELECTUAL:

- CONFIDANTE:

- FUN & ADVENTURE:

- CHICKEN SOUP:

What I can DO and who I can SUPPORT: (Write a short note below about your 'gift' as a person, what you could do to help others, and WHO you know that might need your help.)

MY NOTE ABOUT ME: MY "GIFT" AND HOW I COULD HELP OTHERS (Write it HERE!)

24 - CHOOSING NEXT

We are to the point where another choice is needed. Do we STOP here? Is this the 'last chapter'? Or do we make a plan to move on to something else? Do we have any time left? Or do we have the energy left to do anything else?

We often come to this point and decide to STOP. We don't have a plan to go forward or we can't really think what we want to do or even need to do, so stopping is easy. In the past few years I have worked with a couple fellows who amaze me in the amount and quality of work they can get done in short periods of time. They have a simple plan. If a task is finished, they move to the 'next' one on the list. Of course, that means you have a list of tasks to be done. But you also have the drive to move on down the list.

Some years ago it was fashionable to talk about a "bucket list" and often people would ask, "What's on your bucket list?" Well, bucket list or not, a vision of what comes next or needs to be done next is a good thing to have.

One of the guys I worked with and enjoyed every minute of that time spent, would say "We're burning daylight!" if we had stopped and were standing around for too long. He was ready to move on with the PLAN!

Another man who can do more work than three men in the same amount of time put it another way: "NEXT". When a task or job was done to his satisfaction, and that was usually pretty much to perfection, he would simply say "NEXT" and expect that we would go on to something else that was on a TO DO list.

So, rather than end here, I would like to challenge you to think about this idea. Develop a list of things you need to get done, at work, at home, wherever they might be and have something that you could move on to doing when the task at hand was complete.

No more "burning daylight", just focus on the tasks on the list and move on to the "NEXT" one. Best wishes to you with your CHOOSING and MAINTAINING CONTROL of YOUR LIFE. After all, it IS your life and you get to choose how you spend your 86,400 seconds of every day.

Thanks to my teacher and mentor Dr. William Purkey who would say:

"You've gotta dance like there's nobody watching, Love like you'll never be hurt, Sing like there's nobody listening, And live like it's heaven on earth."
- William W. Purkey

PERSONAL TRIBUTES and THANKS

My sincere expression of Gratitude goes to the following individuals who have played such an important and life-changing role in my life and career as teachers and mentors. I am blessed to know and have known these pioneers in the fields of education, counseling, psychology and psychotherapy. My sincere hope is that their work will never be forgotten or taken for granted. THANKS again and again.

Felice Leonardo "Leo" Buscaglia, Ph.D. (March 31, 1924 – June 12, 1998) former Professor of Special Education at the University of Southern California, internationally known and loved writer, teacher and speaker, who in 1988 received the prestigious Lifetime Achievement Award from The Foundation for Hospice and Homecare for his contributions to a deeper understanding of life, death, joy and love. Leo's favorite quote from "The Little Prince" is below. Thanks for your spirit.

"Here is my secret. It is very simple: It is only with the heart that one can see rightly; what is essential is invisible to the eye."

Le Petit Prince (1943) a novel by Antoine de Saint Exupéry, in English *The Little Prince*.

Robert R. Carkhuff, Ph.D., a world renowned social scientist who has been generating "The Science of Human Generativity" for more than five decades. Best known historically as the father of "The Science of Human Relating," his works include ***Helping and Human Relations, The Development of Human Resources*** *and* ***The Art of Helping,*** now in its 9th edition, has sold more than one million copies and has been translated into numerous languages. Thanks for the visits to "The Mill".

C. H. (Cecil Holden) "Pat" Patterson, Ph.D. (June 22, 1912 – May 26, 2006) Emeritus Professor of Psychology at the University of Illinois at Urbana-Champaign and Professor Emeritus at the University of North Carolina-Greensboro. He worked directly with Dr. Carl Rogers developer of Person Centered Counseling and was a devoted teacher of Rogerian Theory. His second-eldest daughter Francine "Penny" Patterson, a researcher, taught a modified form of American Sign Language to a gorilla named Koko. Thanks for the unconditional positive regard, listening, guidance, genuineness and empathy.

William Watson Purkey, Ed.D., public school teacher, fully tenured professor at the University of Florida, and Professor Emeritus of Counselor Education at the University of North Carolina-Greensboro, he is the co-founder of The International Alliance for Invitational Education and developer of Invitational Counseling theory. Thanks for the invitations to grow.

William Glasser, MD, Psychiatrist, (May 11, 1925 – August 23, 2013) founder of the Institute for Reality Therapy in Los Angeles, California (now the William Glasser Institute, located in Tempe, Arizona) and developer of Reality Therapy and Choice Theory, writer of numerous books on *Reality Therapy, Schools Without Failure,* and *Positive Addiction.* Dr. Glasser advocated the consideration of mental health as a public health issue. In the 1970s, Glasser referred to his body of work as "Control Theory" and in 1996, the theoretical structure evolved into a comprehensive body of work renamed "Choice Theory". Thanks for the hours of role-play and guidance.

Sidney B. Simon, Ed. D. is internationally known for his pioneering work in Values Clarification, now retired as Professor Emeritus from the University of Massachusetts at Amherst, Mass. He has authored over 100 articles and more than a dozen books on values, self-esteem and personal growth and development and conducted many seminars and week-long workshops from Massachusetts to California. His work helped develop a set of practical strategies that have impacted counseling practice, education, social work, medical care and personal growth and development. And, thanks, thanks, thanks for all the personal sharing, support and feedback for the last forty plus years. Without that, where on earth would I be now?

ANOTHER NOTE OF THANKS

I found the following Christmas card recently in one of Leo's books on my shelf and it seemed so appropriate for this time of year to include it here. It has always been a cherished item from a very special mentor and teacher. It goes back to about 1984 but the message is timeless and is a precious example of "writing and talking", as I spoke about earlier in this book, which has lasted for more than thirty years. CHOOSE writing and talking yourself! It lasts! I'm working on my Christmas card list NOW!
December, 2016

Dear Steve,

　　Thank you for the nice card and warm message. Being thought of at this time makes the holidays even more special.

　　"The Perfect Gift" says it all. It was a joy to see!

　　May your life continue to be filled with the magic of love. You are very special!

May your Christmas

BE FILLED WITH

Happiness and Joy

With love,

Leo Buscaglia

For Leo, who loved leaves

Remembering: **The Fall of Freddie the Leaf**, by Dr. Leo Buscaglia, Henry Holt and Co., 1982, NY. The story describes a delicate balance between life and death and is for children and adults of all ages. It is a warm, thought-provoking and comforting story about how Freddie and his leaf friends change as they pass through the seasons and finally move into the final season of winter. This book has meant so much to me in working with grief, death and dying issues over the years. It is recommended reading.

ACKNOWLEDGEMENTS AND BOOK LIST

Over my life and career, I have found these works to be essential parts of my personal and professional development. My approach to teaching and therapy has been deeply seated in the teachings and writings of these individuals. Personal relationships and information sharing with these individuals has directly impacted who I am today. Without these individuals and this knowledge, I am not sure just where I would be today and how I would have done this work. For this connection and support, I am eternally grateful.

Aspy, David, and Roebuck, F.N. *KIDS Don't Learn From People They Don't Like,* Amherst, Mass: Human Resource Development Press, 1977.

Buscaglia, Leo *Love*, New York: Fawcett Crest, 1972

Buscaglia, Leo *Living, Loving & Learning,* New York: Fawcett Columbine, 1982

Buscaglia, Leo *Loving each Other,* New York: Hold, Rinehart and Winston, 1984

Carkhuff, Robert *The Art of Helping,* Amherst, Mass: Human Resource Development Press, 1983, 2009

Carkhuff, Robert, Bernard Berenson and Rob Owen, *The Secrets of Helping,* Amherst, Mass: HRD Press. 2009

Carkhuff, Robert, Bernard Berenson, Jeannette Tamagini, *The Heart of Empathy,* Amherst, Mass: HRD Press 2014

Glasser, William, *Reality Therapy: A New Approach to Psychiatry,* New York: Harper & Row, Publishers, 1965

Glasser, William *Positive Addiction,* New York: Harper & Row, 1976

Glasser, William *Take Effective Control of Your Life,* New York: Harper & Row, 1984

Glasser, William *Choice Theory,* New York: Harper Collins, 1998

Paterson, C. H. *The Therapeutic Relationship: Foundations for an Eclectic Psychotherapy,* Belmont, CA: Wadsworth Publishing Inc., 1985

Patterson, C. H. *Theories of Counseling and Psychotherapy,* New York: Harper & Row, 1986

Patterson, C. H. *Understanding Psychotherapy: Fifty Years of Client-Centered Theory and Practice,* Herefordshire: United Kingdom, PCCS Books, 2000

Purkey, William and John Novak *Inviting School Success,* Belmont, CA: Wadsworth Publishing Co., 1984

Simon, Sidney B., Leland Howe, and Howard Kirschenbaum, *Values Clarification,* New York: Dodd, Mead & Co., 1972

Simon, Sidney *Meeting Yourself Halfway,* Amherst, Mass: Edit, Inc., 1974

Simon, Sidney *Getting Unstuck,* New York: Warner Books, 1988

Simon, Sidney and Suzanne Simon *Forgiveness,* New York: Warner Communications, 1990

Wubbolding, Robert *Understanding Reality Therapy*, New York: Harper Collins, 1991

Wubbolding, Robert *Using Reality Therapy.* New York: Harper Collins, 1998

Wubbolding, Robert *Reality Therapy,* Washington DC: American Psychological Association, 2011

Thanks to my good friend and confidante Matthew Casey McBrayer, III, who taught me that: **"The MAIN Thing Is to Maintain"**.

ABOUT THE AUTHOR

Steve J. Leatherwood, MA, LPC, NCC, began working as a psychologist at Western Carolina Center in 1970 following graduation from Western Carolina University with a BA in Psychology/Social Science. He later obtained an MA in Psychology from Appalachian State University and continued post-graduate education in Greensboro, NC at UNC-G. Since 1970, Leatherwood has worked consistently in the field of mental health counseling and psychotherapy. In the 1970's, he became Director of Psychological Services at Cleveland County Mental Health Center and was an adjunct professor of Psychology at Gardner-Webb University for thirty years. He is certified in Reality Therapy by Dr. William Glasser. In addition, Leatherwood has maintained a private practice in counseling and employee assistance programs since 1975 which has continued to the present time. His focus for much of his career has been in working with children and adolescents, family and marriage counseling and anger/anxiety management. He has been married since 1968 to his high school sweetheart, Dotty, and they have two adult sons. Fun activities include playing music, especially bluegrass, woodworking and 'tinkering' with old cars and trucks. At this point, he has no real desire to 'grow up' any more, just to grow older.

"Grown-ups never understand anything by themselves, and it is tiresome for children to be always and forever explaining things to them."

Le Petit Prince (1943) a novel by Antoine de Saint Exupéry, translated into English as **The Little Prince**.

YOUR NOTES AND PERSONAL THOUGHTS